Time Capsule

Written by Frank Pedersen
Illustrated by Debe Mansfield

Contents	Page
Chapter 1. *A meteor shower*	4
Chapter 2. *An alien object?*	10
Chapter 3. *Welcome to my world*	18
Chapter 4. *Past mistakes*	23
Chapter 5. *A request is made*	27
Chapter 6. *Forty years later...*	30
Verse	32

Time Capsule

With these characters . . .

Sarah Mitchell

Someone From The Future

"Welcom

Setting the scene . . .

While watching a spectacular meteor shower, Sarah Mitchell has no idea that, very soon, she will have to make a choice that will affect the lives of everyone on the planet. A mysterious object falls from the sky and, while her father and grandmother are not looking, Sarah manages to unlock its secrets. A terrible shock is in store, however, and an amazing series of events unfolds on Sarah's computer screen as she meets someone from a strange and scary future.

o my world, Sarah Mitchell!"

Chapter 1.

Sarah Mitchell lay staring at the night sky. Her mat was thick enough to keep the dampness of the ground away from her back but not thick enough to dull the sharp points of the stones underneath. The trees around her were black shadows, and the air was still. The astronomers on the radio had forecast a fabulous meteor shower between 10:00 and 11:00 P.M.—but an hour was a long time to wait with stones pressing into your back.

Without warning, a streak of light across the sky heralded the start of the meteor shower. Instantly, Sarah forgot all about her discomfort and gazed at the sky. A few moments later, there was another speeding line of light as a second meteor burned up in the Earth's atmosphere, then another, and another. Soon, the night sky was ablaze with streaking meteors hurtling across the sky. As the astronomers had predicted, this meteor shower was the best!

Sarah had counted about thirty meteors when she noticed another curious light rapidly growing brighter and brighter. Within seconds, it was a burning, red-hot spot speeding her way! Sarah's heart thumped faster. She gasped. This was no ordinary meteor. This wasn't shooting across the sky! It was diving directly downward—to where she lay!

The meteor was approaching at thousands of miles an hour. Sarah froze. There was nowhere to run and no time to do anything. Seconds later, the whole field lit up like a floodlit football field. An enormous crash rocked the ground where Sarah lay terrified.

It was a whole minute before Sarah dared to move. Slowly, she raised herself up from the mat and looked over to where the meteor had crashed into the ground. A dull red light glowed from the dirt.

Steam and smoke rose from the edge of the field. A strange burning smell wafted over the field. Sarah trembled, not knowing what she should do next.

She looked around and saw that light was streaming out of her grandmother's house in the next field. People were running toward her, shouting her name.

"I'm OK," she called shakily to her grandmother and her father. "I'm OK, really."

Both grown-ups reached her panting and puffing. They hugged her tightly.

"What on Earth ...?" said her father, staring at the red glow by the fence with its rising clouds of smoke.

"What's that smell?" asked her grandmother, sniffing the smoky air.

"I think a meteor fell to Earth," replied Sarah, brushing her hair out of her eyes.

Her grandmother's eyes widened in amazement. "Are you sure you're alright?" she said, looking very worried.

Sarah nodded and pointed to the edge of the field. "It missed me, but it was pretty close!"

Treading cautiously, the family made its way across the bumpy field to where the meteor had hit.

They saw a huge hole, as big as a car, with dirt piled up around its edge. The grass around the hole was blackened and charred. As she got closer, Sarah could see that the red glow was not constant, but was blinking like the flash of a police car's lights. Holding her father's hand tightly, she peered over the edge. Sarah was stunned by what she saw. This was no meteor.

Chapter 2.

At the base of the hole lay a long, cylindrical object. Although it was blackened by heat, Sarah could tell that it was made of metal. On top of the cylinder a clear red light was flashing like a beacon. On one side of the cylinder was a row of ten tiny buttons.

"Aliens!" wailed her grandmother. "People from Mars waiting to attack us all!"

"I don't think so," said Sarah's father. "Not unless they use the same number system as we do." He pointed at the row of buttons. Beside each one was a number from zero to nine. "Maybe it's a piece of a satellite that fell out of its orbit," he suggested. "That does happen, you know. Only, they usually drop into the ocean unnoticed."

Sarah's grandmother's expression changed from fear to annoyance. If this *was* from a satellite, she would have words with someone. How dare they drop their satellite onto her farm without permission! The nerve of it!

Sarah and her father knew *that* expression.

"Now, come on, Grandma," said Sarah's father. "We don't want to cause trouble for anyone until the morning, do we? Let's leave this here and call the police first thing tomorrow."

Sarah and her father walked back up the field to the house, the long grass brushing against their legs. Sarah's grandmother followed muttering threats about complaining to the local council. "Satellites!" she murmured. "Trespassing on my farm!"

The next morning, Sarah's father walked into the kitchen, carrying the cylinder wrapped up in Sarah's damp mat. In all the excitement, she had left it out all night. With a thump, he placed it on the table. Perspiration dripped off his forehead as he unwrapped the cylinder.

"It's heavy, whatever it is," he said.

Sarah and her grandmother studied the strange piece of satellite wreckage. The metal casing was smooth except for the buttons with numbers. There appeared to be no way to open it. The red light had stopped blinking. The cylinder had no doors, joints, or hinges.

"I'd better call the police," said Sarah's father, as he left to use the telephone in the hallway.

"I'm coming with you," said her grandmother. "I want to have a word with whoever is in charge of that!" She pointed at the cylinder angrily.

Sarah was left with the cylinder. Running her hand over its cool, smooth surface, she looked at the buttons. She pressed one, and swiftly drew back her hand. Nothing happened. She pressed another. Still nothing.

After pressing another four buttons, she almost jumped through the ceiling when the red light flashed. Then it died out again.

Suddenly, Sarah realized what it was. "It needs a PIN number, just like a money machine or a bank card," she thought. Quickly, she punched in another six numbers, and held her breath. The light flashed red once more. Then she had an idea.

"Why not?" she thought, grinning playfully. She punched in the date of her birthday. 0-6-0-1-1-9-9-1.

The light flashed. Sarah gasped. She felt a stab of fear. This time, the light was flashing green!

A tiny compartment hidden in the cylinder silently slid open. Sarah stared in astonishment. She half expected something alive to crawl out and attack her. Luckily, there was nothing strange or alien inside. Within the compartment was a bright, sparkling CD. Shaking with excitement, Sarah plucked it out. Under the CD, in bold, red letters, was a notice. It said:

"CLOSE IMMEDIATELY!"

Sarah pushed the edge of the compartment door, which vanished into the smooth cylinder without a trace.

Sarah hurriedly hid the CD in her pocket, as she heard her father and grandmother approaching from the hallway. Later, she planned to investigate this disc in secret, without any interference from grown-ups, the police, or whomever Dad had called.

For the rest of the day, Sarah found it difficult to hide her excitement.

She lingered around her father's study, waiting for him to finish working on his computer so that she could check the CD. But he was busy writing for most of the day. It was not until after dinner, when her father and her grandmother were watching television, that she could sneak into the study and switch on the computer.

With her heart thumping, Sarah waited until the computer had booted up. Then she pressed the eject button, and the disc tray slid open. She placed the mysterious CD in the tray and watched it slide into the computer.

After a few seconds, the CD stopped whirring and a strange symbol appeared on the screen. Underneath it was written "Click Me."

Sarah hesitated as she moved the mouse pointer to the strange icon.

"Oh, well," she thought, as she clicked on the icon. "Here goes."

Slowly, the blue screen in front of her dissolved, and a disturbing image began to take shape on the screen. It started out as a picture of the countryside with trees and streams and blue skies.

Then it turned into what looked like a picture of the Moon or Mars, except everything was brown, instead of gray or red.

Then Sarah got the shock of her life! A message slowly appeared on screen. But it was a most disturbing message. She stared at the last two words in disbelief.

"Welcome to my world, Sarah Mitchell!" it read.
How could this be? Who had sent her this CD? Where had this strange CD come from? Sarah's mind was filled with questions. She sat gazing at the screen, wondering if she was dreaming.

Then another icon appeared below the message. "Click to Proceed," it said.

Chapter 3.

Sarah clicked on the icon.

Suddenly, the computer's speakers burst into life. The study was filled with loud sounds of birds singing, running water, and rustling leaves. Sarah reached quickly for the volume control. But it was too late.

"What's that noise?" called her father from the living room.

"I'm just playing a computer game," replied Sarah shakily. She crept over and closed the door, in case there were more surprises.

When she returned to the computer, some new text had appeared on the screen. Sarah sat there, fascinated by what she read. This was no computer game. This was for real.

"The sounds you are hearing are from our audio-museums," read the text. "No one in our world has heard these sounds for many years. We can only remember what it was like to live in a world where the birds sang, water ran in rivers, and air rustled the leaves on trees."

"Today, most of our animals and plants are extinct."

The screen turned bright blue and a golden yellow circle in the corner lit up a new section of text.

"No one born into our world knows what it is like to look up into a clear blue sky or to feel the warmth of our sun on their skin," it said.

Suddenly, the brilliant blue screen turned a muddy brown. The yellow circle became a hazy, red dot. The sounds of birds, water, and wind grew faint and then faded into silence.

"This is our world. A world where our environment is too dangerous for us to live outside. A world where our bodies are under constant attack from pollution, radiation, and harmful new strains of bacteria."

Then Sarah stared at the line beneath. It flashed ominously at her, in large, red letters.

"In a few short years, this may be *your* world, too."

Sarah was horrified. How could it be *her* world?

Two icons appeared on the screen. One said "Quit." The other said "Continue." Sarah clicked "Continue."

A video image appeared. A figure in a white spacesuit seemed to be nodding at Sarah.

"I am glad you chose to continue," said the figure in a crackly voice. The CD whirred and clicked as the on-screen video played. "You obviously care about your planet."

"Many years ago, we breathed clean air and drank clean water. Animals, birds, and plants lived here. We enjoyed comfortable homes and lived long, healthy lives. We designed great, new technology. Little did we know that we were destroying our planet."

"No one noticed when things first started to go wrong. And, when they did, everyone thought it was someone *else's* problem to fix. No one wanted to change the way they lived. And, all around them, things were getting worse every day."

"As we used more and more energy, our atmosphere began to heat up. Slowly, our seasons changed, and it became harder and harder to grow our food crops. Even the polar icecaps began melting, threatening to flood our earth. Our world was drastically out of balance."

The figure in white stared straight out of the screen at Sarah.

"Listen carefully, Sarah Mitchell!"

Chapter 4.

Sarah felt compelled to listen even though the story upset her.

"As we cleared forests and built more and more factories, our air became dirtier. As we built more and more vehicles, we emitted more pollution. Slowly, the chemical pollution reacted with the water in our atmosphere and our rain became more acidic. The acid rain slowly caused our trees and plants to stop growing, and then they died."

"Still, no one cared. They all thought someone else would come up with a solution. They thought it wasn't *their* problem."

"Eventually, the soil and water that we depended upon became poisonous. Our normal crops could not grow. We had to build even bigger factories to produce food in an artificial environment. This just made the problem worse."

The figure in white moved to one side of the screen, and a graph appeared on the other side.

"Once, our planet supported hundreds of thousands of species of plants and animals."

"Today, only a few remain. We preserve them in special buildings where heat, water, and light are carefully controlled. But our efforts were too little, too late. The rest of our planet is ruined."

Sarah sat back in her chair. This was terrible! The CD whirred and clicked in the disc drive again, and a new picture appeared on screen.

It was a brown planet, circled by an orange haze.

"Now it is too late for us to do anything. The problem is too big for us to solve. Even in your time, Sarah Mitchell, it is a huge task. But you can take action. Without action now, this will be *your* world in a few short years."

The figure in white reappeared and slowly unbuttoned the spacesuit.

The figure removed the helmet and Sarah slumped back in shock. The person's face looked strangely familiar; she was a woman about fifty years old, with the same skin, eyes, and hair as Sarah's grandmother—but, in some ways, she looked different.

"We may be able to survive on this planet for only another year or two," said the woman grimly. "Despite our technology, our food supplies are growing short. It is getting harder and harder to clean the air and water that we need to survive in our shelters. We need your help—now."

"There is much work to do. But I know that I can trust you to work as hard as you can over the following years to save your planet."

The woman smiled.

"How do I know? Because I know all about you, Sarah Mitchell, and I know what you are capable of."

Sarah nearly jumped out of her chair. How did this woman know all about her? Who was she? Had she been spying on Sarah?

The woman reached into her spacesuit pocket and brought out a small, faded card. She held it in front of her and stepped forward so that it filled the screen.

Sarah looked at the card and, with shivers running down her back, realized what it was—a driver's license. There was a photo of the woman on it. But worse, much worse, was the name and birth date beside the photo: Sarah Mitchell January 6th, 1991.

Chapter 5.

Sarah Mitchell was stunned. She stared at the computer screen. Her heart was racing. As she studied the woman's face again, she wondered if this was really her own face in forty years time.

"Sarah, there is much to explain. But it will take time," said the woman. "If you wish to save your planet, you must copy the contents of this CD onto your hard drive. This CD contains information about all the bad decisions, mistakes, and actions that will be taken on Earth over the next forty years. All the information you will need to change the way things turn out is here—but you must *want* to help. You must be prepared to work for many years, using this information to change the way people behave. You must trust me."

The woman smiled.

"Sarah Mitchell, you must trust yourself. You have ten seconds to decide."

Two more icons appeared on screen. One said "Delete." The other said "Copy."

Sarah's hand rested on the mouse. She wavered between the two icons. This was too scary. Maybe she should call her father for help. Maybe she should wait until the police arrived to pick up the strange cylinder. At the top of the screen, a tiny clock appeared, counting down the seconds.

"10 ... 9 ... 8 ..."

Sarah was petrified. *Was this really a message from the future? What should she do? Trust this stranger who claimed to be her? Believe the terrible story that she had told?*

"7 ... 6 ... 5 ..."

Seconds raced past. Sarah's eyes were fixed on the clock. Her hand tightened on the mouse. She thought about the story she'd heard on the CD. She thought about the things that she knew were happening to the environment.

Surely, *someone* would find a solution to the problem before it all went terribly wrong. Why did it have to be *her*?

"4 … 3 … 2 …"

Sarah felt a rising wave of panic. When time was up, she moved the mouse pointer over an icon, closed her eyes, and clicked.

Chapter 6.

Forty years passed. Sarah Mitchell sat alone in her study working on the last part of a computer program. The curtain was drawn and the only light came from a small desk lamp beside the computer. Sarah stretched. The work she had been doing every day for the last ten years was almost complete. She slumped back in her chair and gazed toward the window. Finally, she turned back to her computer, and pressed the "Record" button. A shiny new CD clicked and whirred in her disc drive.

What kind of world lay beyond those curtains? If Sarah had made a different decision all those years ago, the scene outside the window would be very different from what it was today. Sarah closed her eyes and remembered a time when she had sat in front of another computer, watching as a tiny clock had ticked away the seconds. If, all those years ago, she had clicked on the *other* icon, what might have happened?

She would never know.

As the CD hummed and whirred in the disc drive, Sarah stood up and paced around the room. The world that lay outside her window would have looked very different if she had made a different choice.

Sarah Mitchell stopped in front of the window. She reached out and flung open the curtain to look at the world outside. Which icon had she chosen?

"A message slowly appeared on screen."

With ten short seconds
Left to go,
You're asked to change
The world you know!

In your trembling hands,
the planet's fate!
What sort of world
Will you create?

Look out your window,
What do you see?
A world full of life—
Or not a single tree?